SimNet XPe
PageOut
Release 3.1

MW01144306

Computer-Based Learning and Assessment for

Microsoft® Office XP
(Microsoft® Word 2002)
(Microsoft® Excel 2002)
(Microsoft® Access 2002)
(Microsoft® PowerPoint® 2002)

Microsoft® Windows® 2000 Professional

Microsoft® FrontPage® 2002

Computer Concepts

Microsoft® Windows® XP Professional

Microsoft® Internet Explorer™ 6

Integrating Microsoft® Office XP

by Triad Interactive, Inc.

Published by McGraw-Hill/Technology Education, an imprint of the McGraw-Hill Companies, Inc. 1221 Avenue of the Americas, New York, NY 10020. Copyright © 2003 by the McGraw-Hill Companies. All rights reserved. No part of this publication may be reproduced or distributed in any form or by any means, or stored in a database or retrieval system, without the prior written consent of The McGraw-Hill Companies, Inc., including, but not limited to, in any network or other electronic storage or transmission, or broadcast for distance learning.

Contents

APPROVED COURSEWARE

MOUS Approved Courseware

What does this logo mean?

It means this courseware has been approved by the Microsoft® Office User Specialist Program to be among the finest available for learning _Microsoft Word 2002, Microsoft Excel 2002, Microsoft Access 2002, Microsoft PowerPoint 2002, and Microsoft FrontPage 2002_. It also means that upon completion of this courseware, you may be prepared to become a Microsoft Office User Specialist. SimNet XPert is approved courseware to prepare you for the MOUS Core Level Exam and the Expert Level Exam.

What is a Microsoft Office User Specialist?

A Microsoft Office User Specialist is an individual who has certified his or her skills in one or more of the Microsoft Office desktop applications of Microsoft Word, Microsoft Excel, Microsoft PowerPoint®, Microsoft Outlook® or Microsoft Access, or in Microsoft Project. The Microsoft Office User Specialist Program typically offers certification exams at the "Core" and "Expert" skill levels. *   The Microsoft Office User Specialist Program is the only Microsoft approved program in the world for certifying proficiency in Microsoft Office desktop applications and Microsoft Project. This certification can be a valuable asset in any job search or career advancement.

More Information:

To learn more about becoming a Microsoft Office User Specialist, visit www.mous.net

To purchase a Microsoft Office User Specialist certification exam, visit www.DesktopIQ.com

To learn about other Microsoft Office User Specialist approved courseware from McGraw-Hill/Irwin, visit http://www.mhhe.com/catalogs/irwin/cit/mous/index.mhtml

* The availability of Microsoft Office User Specialist certification exams varies by application, application version, and language. Visit www.mous.net for exam availability.

Microsoft, the Microsoft Office User Specialist Logo, PowerPoint and Outlook are either registered trademarks or trademarks of Microsoft Corporation in the United States and/or other countries.

SimNet XPert Combined PageOut® Edition, Release 3.1

System Requirements

- Windows 98 SE, Windows Me, Windows 2000 Professional, Windows XP Professional or Home

- Internet Explorer 5.5 (included on CD)

- Windows Media Player 7.0 (included on CD)

- Pentium II or higher with minimum 300 MHz processor

- 64 MB RAM

- We (and Microsoft) recommend 128 MB RAM with Windows XP

- CD-ROM drive

- Internet connection (for PageOut® access)

- Sound card and speakers (for audio narration)

- *Live Application Exams* require installation of Office XP with medium or low macro security. (We do not recommend low macro security.)

- **IMPORTANT NOTE**: **Allowing Cookies for PageOut®**. In order to access SimNet XPert Lessons and/or Exams from a PageOut® course web site you must set your browser to allow third-party cookies from PageOut®. For more information on the type of cookie used by PageOut®, and for instructions on how to configure your browser to accept cookies from PageOut®, refer to the section later in this manual called *Security, Cookies, and PageOut®*.

Installing SimNet XPert

IMPORTANT NOTE: You must uninstall any prior version of SimNet (**SimNet 2000, SimNet 2.0, or SimNet XPert**) that you may have installed on your computer before installing this version of **SimNet XPert**. You can do so either by running the uninstall program that was added to your SimNet program manager group (under the Start-> Programs->SimNet menu option) or by using *Add/Remove Programs* under the Control Panel (Start->Settings->Control Panel).

The installation program for **SimNet XPert** will run automatically (if your CD-ROM drive is set to autorun) when you insert the **SimNet XPert Disk 1** CD-ROM into your CD-ROM drive. If it does not begin automatically, double-click My Computer, and then double-click the icon for your CD-ROM drive (with the **SimNet XPert Disk 1** CD in that drive).

The installation program checks whether you have the most recent version of Windows Media Player installed (which is required for the audio narration you will hear when you run the *Show Me's* in **SimNet XPert Learning**, and either of the *Product Tours*). If you do not have the most recent version of Windows Media Player, the installation program will prompt you to proceed with an installation of the Windows Media Player 7.1. We recommend you accept the defaults in this installation program with the possible exception of making Media Player your default player for all related file types. For **SimNet XPert** you need the Media Player to be the default player for *.wma* files. If you are installing Windows Media Player, your computer must reboot, after which the installation program will continue to the **SimNet XPert** install. If the installation program does not restart automatically, double-click My Computer, and then double-click the icon for your CD-ROM drive (with the **SimNet XPert Disk 1** CD in that drive). You must allow the **SimNet XPert** installation to complete before you can begin using **SimNet XPert**.

For a step-by-step walk-through of the installation process, refer to *Appendix A: SimNet XPert Installation Walk-Through*.

Installation for SimNet XPert

Once you have the most recent version of Windows Media Player installed, you will see dialog boxes indicating you are ready to install **SimNet XPert**. We recommend you accept the defaults displaying during this process, although you are free to change them if you'd like. If the installation program does not restart automatically, double-click My Computer, and then double-click the icon for your CD-ROM drive (with the **SimNet XPert Disk 1** CD in that drive). You must allow the **SimNet XPert** installation to complete before you can begin using **SimNet XPert**. For a step-by-step walk-through of the installation process, refer to *Appendix A: SimNet XPert Installation Walk-Through*.

Quick-Start Instructions

Although we strongly recommend that you read the instructions in this manual, we appreciate the fact that often this just isn't possible. We are therefore including these Quick-Start Instructions which cover the absolute minimum number of steps required to begin using SimNet XPert. No screen shots are included in this section of the manual, and there is no discussion of various options that might be available to you. These are strictly the fewest steps necessary to begin using SimNet XPert.

Starting SimNet XPert

1. With either Disk 1 or Disk 2 in your CD-ROM drive, click on the Start button on the Windows taskbar
2. Select Programs from the Start Menu
3. Select SimNet XPert from the Programs Menu
4. Select either Disk 1 or Disk 2 from the SimNet XPert Menu.

Taking a SimNet XPert PageOut® Lesson

1. Either identify where your *My Lessons* folder resides, or cancel that step
2. Click the **Take a Lesson** button
3. Click the **PageOut® Lessons** button
4. Choose which type of lesson you wish to access by clicking the appropriate button
5. Click the **SimNet XPert** menu link on your instructor's course web site
6. Click the name of the lesson you wish to access and click the **Select Lesson** button
7. Click the on the desired folder in the lesson navigation pane
8. Click the name of the desired skill or topic
9. Go through the Teach Me, Show Me, and Let Me Try for that skill or topic

Taking a SimNet XPert PageOut® Exam

1. Either identify where your *My Lessons* folder resides, or cancel that step
2. Click the **Take an Exam** button
3. Click the **PageOut® Exams** button
4. Type your instructor's PageOut® URL into the box provided and click the **Log In** button

5. Click the **SimNet XPert** menu link on your instructor's course web site

6. Click the name of the exam you wish to access and click the **Select Exam** button

7. Answer the questions as they appear in the question box for the exam

8. Click the **End Test** button when finished

Running SimNet XPert

Important note: BEFORE YOU BEGIN SimNet XPert

In SimNet XPert Combined you are able to have the program create custom lessons for you. These custom lessons can be created when you have completed a SimNet XPert exam. In order to save these custom lessons you need to create a folder either on your computer's hard drive (or a mapped network drive to which you have write permissions) or have a pre-formatted floppy disk. The folder must be named *My Lessons*. If you do not have this folder already created, on either a hard drive or a floppy disk, SimNet XPert will not be able to save your custom lessons. You will need to remember where you create your *My Lessons* folder as you will need to identify the location when you log into SimNet XPert. For more on custom lessons, refer to the section with the same name (**Custom Lessons**) later in this manual.

Important note on the two disks for SimNet XPert

SimNet XPert Combined Release 3.1 comes on two disks. Each disk contains all of the content (both Learning and Assessment) for the modules listed below.

Disk 1: Access 2002
       Excel 2002
       PowerPoint 2002
       Word 2002
       Office XP Integration
       Windows 2000 Professional

Disk 2: FrontPage 2002
       Computer Concepts
       Internet Explorer 6
       Windows XP Professional

Starting SimNet XPert

Once you have successfully completed the installation process, you can start SimNet XPert by one of these two methods:

1. Insert either Disk 1 or Disk 2, depending on which content you wish to access, and use the Autorun menu that appears (if your CD-ROM drive is set to autorun). If the autorun menu does not appear automatically when you insert the disk, use the method below.

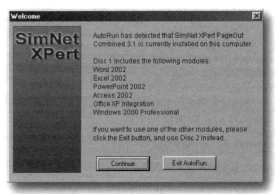

SimNet XPert Disk 1 Autorun Check Screen

2. With either Disk 1 or Disk 2, depending on which content you wish to access, already in your CD-ROM drive, click on the Start button on the Windows taskbar. From the Start menu select Programs, and from the Programs Menu select SimNet XPert. From the SimNet XPert menu select either SimNet XPert 3.1 Disk 1 or SimNet XPert 3.1 Disk 2, depending on which disk you have in your CD-ROM drive.

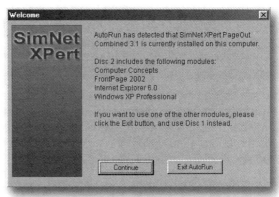

SimNet XPert Disk 2 Autorun Check Screen

The first dialog box that appears checks to ensure you want to access the modules on that disk. If you have started from the correct disk, click the **Continue** button.

The subsequent dialog box displays the AutoRun menu. You can:

• run the Student program by clicking on the first button,

• uninstall the Student program by clicking the fifth button, or

• exit the program by clicking the bottom button.

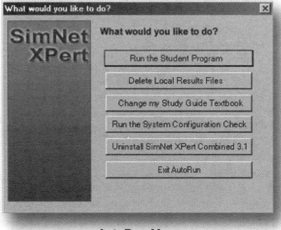

AutoRun Menu

Identifying the location for "My Lessons"

As soon as you have logged in, a dialog box appears asking you to identify where the program can save and locate any custom lessons for you. Custom lessons can be created automatically after you complete a SimNet XPert exam. (When you finish the exam and the results report is displayed, you can click the **Make Custom Lesson** button to have SimNet XPert assemble a lesson that covers the skills or topic you did not get correct on that exam.) If you want to access

The choose a "My Lessons" folder dialog box

any of your previously-created Custom Lessons, or if you want SimNet XPert to save any Custom Lessons you will have created, you need to identify the folder on your hard drive (or a floppy disk) where the Custom Lessons reside. If you click Cancel you will still be able to use all other functionality in the product; you just won't be able to retrieve any previously-created Custom Lesson.

In the dialog box you need to navigate to the location of your "My Lessons" folder. (Clicking on the + sign expands the drive to show the folders on that drive). If your "My Lessons" folder resides within another folder, continue clicking on the + sign on the appropriate drive until you see the folder name. Then click on your "My Lessons" folder and click the OK button.

For more on Custom Lessons, refer to the section *Make Custom Lessons* later in this manual.

Choosing where to go

After successfully logging into SimNet XPert Combined, you will see the SimNet XPert Student Program Main Menu. Regardless of which disk you are using, there are three buttons available:

Take an Exam: clicking this button opens the Assessment Component of SimNet XPert Combined from which you can access exams and tests.

Take a Lesson: clicking this button opens the Learning Component of SimNet XPert Combined from which you can access computer-based tutorials.

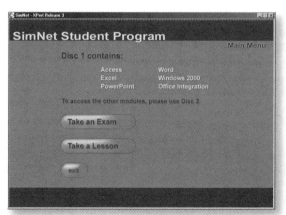

Disk 1 Main Menu

Exit: clicking this button terminates SimNet XPert Combined.

Special Note about Disk 1 and Disk 2

Be sure to insert the correct disk to access the content you desire. The content breakdown is as follows:

Disk 1: Access 2002
Excel 2002
PowerPoint 2002
Word 2002
Office XP Integration
Windows 2000
Professional

Disk 2: FrontPage 2002
Computer Concepts
Internet Explorer 6
Windows XP
Professional

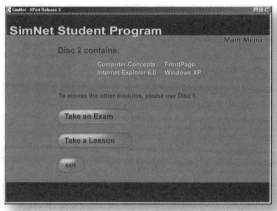

Disk 2 Main Menu

SimNet XPert Learning

Learning Component Main Menu

The *SimNet XPert Learning* Main Menu opens after you click the **Take a Lesson** button. There are three types of lessons available:

1. The *Learning* module Main Menu opens with the **Office Specialist Lessons** displayed in the lesson list box. These are pre-installed lessons organized by Microsoft Office (User) Specialist objective.

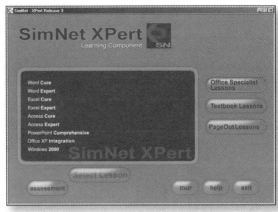

Disk 1 Learning Main Menu without the My Lessons button

2. If your instructor has assigned a McGraw-Hill textbook to your class, you can click the **Textbook Lessons** button to see the list of available textbooks. If you are an independent student, you will not have the textbook lessons available.

3. The **PageOut Lessons** button is used to access your instructor's PageOut® course web site. From the course web site you will be able to access customized lessons assigned by your instructor. You will need to be online to use the PageOut® Lessons button. For instructions on Loading a Lesson from your instructor's PageOut® course web site, see the section below called *Loading a Lesson from PageOut®*.

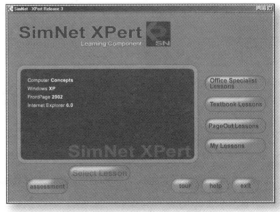

Disk 2 Learning Main Menu with the My Lessons button

4. If you identified the location of the *My Lessons* folder after first logging into SimNet XPert, there will be a fourth button: **My Lessons**. Clicking on this button displays a list of the custom lessons that have been created for you.

To begin a lesson, click a lesson title. Lessons can take a minute or two to load, be patient if nothing happens at first. You should see a **Loading Lessons...** screen within 30 seconds or so.

The *Learning* Main Menu includes an **Assessment** button. You can click this button to go to the *Assessment* program. (In the *Assessment* program, there is a **Learning** button which you can use to switch back to the *Learning* program.)

Loading a Lesson from PageOut®

Click the **PageOut® Lessons** button on the Learning Component main menu.

1. Type the **PageOut®** address supplied by your instructor, and then click the **Log In** button. Note that all **PageOut®** addresses end in *.pageout.net*, which is already on the log in screen, so all you need to type is whatever precedes *.pageout.net* in the address supplied by your instructor.

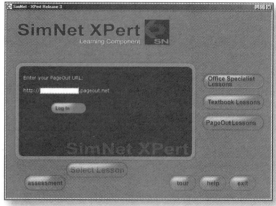

Launching SimNet XPert PageOut® Edition

2. Click the link for your **PageOut®** course from your instructor's **PageOut®** web site home page.

At the instructor's PageOut® Course Web Site

3. Click **SimNet XPert** in the navigation menu at the left side of the next page displayed (or at the bottom of that page), the Course Home Page.

A course home page with SimNet XPert link

4. At the next screen enter your User ID and Password. You should have either received these from your instructor, or you should have been allowed to self-register, in which case you created your own User ID and Password.

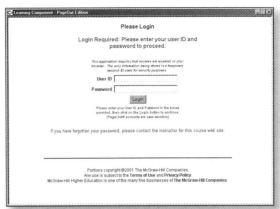

The PageOut® Login Screen

5. After logging in successfully you will have access to a menu of lessons (and possibly exams) created by your instructor for you to access. Clicking on an active lesson will load that lesson on your screen. This may take a few moments, depending on your Internet connection.

A brief SimNet XPert menu in PageOut®

Overview of Lessons

Each lesson opens with the *Progress Review* on the right and the navigation menu on the left. When you start a new lesson, all entries in the *Progress Review* show "not completed."

Scoring

Skills are recorded as "completed" when you click the **Finish** button at the end of the *Let Me Try* exercise. Your progress report is saved and sent to the Instructor program automatically.

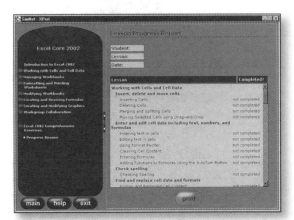

Opening Lesson Screen

Navigating SimNet XPert Learning

To navigate the skills in the lesson, click a folder in the Navigation menu. If the lesson is a custom lesson created by your instructor, there will be only one folder. If the lesson is one of the pre-installed Microsoft Office (User) Specialist or textbook lessons, there may be multiple folders. If necessary, click a subfolder to expand it to see the list of skills.

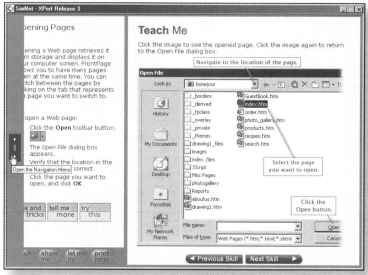

Opening the Navigation Pane

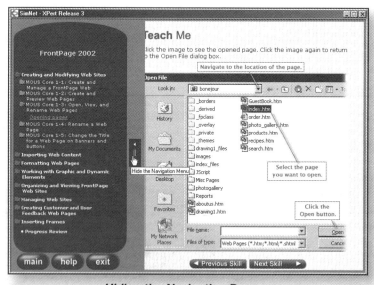

Hiding the Navigation Pane

Skills appear as underlined titles in the Navigation menu. Click a title to open it.

To go to another skill, click the **Next Skill** or **Previous Skill** button at the bottom of the *Teach Me* or *Show Me* window. Or, expand the navigation menu, and click another skill title.

In *SimNet XPert Learning*, each skill has three parts: **Teach Me**, **Show Me**, and **Let Me Try**. The *Teach Me* section opens automatically. To print the *Teach Me* text, click the **Print** button at the bottom of the window.

Teach Me

Each *Teach Me* section includes a brief explanation of the skill and step-by-step instructions. Many of the *Teach Me's* include interactivity in the right-hand pane of the screen. Some *Teach Me's* include further information at the end of the text. Click each of the buttons to see the information in a pop-up window.

- Click the **Tips and Tricks** button for related information about the skill.

- Click the **Tell Me More** button for further information and advanced techniques.

- Click the **Try This** button for alternate methods such as menu commands and keyboard shortcuts.

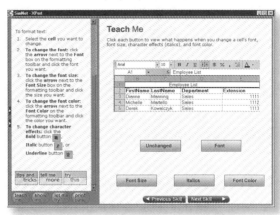

Teach Me with interactivity in the right-hand pane

Show Me

The *Show Me* section includes step-by-step instructions and an animation with audio narration showing how to complete the skill. Click the **Start** button to play the animation. Click the **Caption** button to display text of the narration.

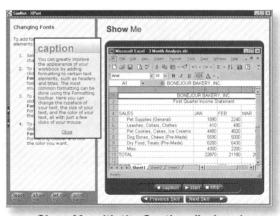

Show Me with the Caption displayed

Let Me Try

The *Let Me Try* exercise utilizes the simulated application interface. Answer the question by completing the appropriate action. The program will tell you if your response was correct or incorrect. If correct, you move on to the next question. If incorrect, you can try again. You must complete each step correctly before moving on.

If you have trouble completing a step, click the **Hint** at the bottom of the question box.

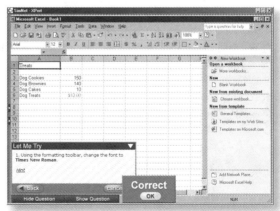

Let Me Try after answering first question correctly

13

Hiding and Showing the Question Box

You can hide the question box by clicking the **Hide Question** button or clicking the minimize arrow at the top right corner of the question box. Click the **Show Question** button to display the question again. If you "lose" the question box, just click the **Show Question** button to show the question box again.

You can also move the question box to another part of the window by clicking the title bar, then dragging the box to its new location. See the section: *Working with the Question Box* later in this manual for more details.

Comprehensive Exercises

Some lessons may contain *Comprehensive Exercises*. *Comprehensive Exercises* are *Let Me Try* exercises that encompass multiple skills. They don't have a *Teach Me* or *Show Me* section. Click the **Start Exercise** button to begin the *Comprehensive Exercise*.

Progress Review

To check your progress, click **Progress Review** at the bottom of the navigation menu. Skills are recorded as "completed" when you click the **Finish** button at the end of the *Let Me Try* exercises. Your progress review is saved and sent to the Instructor Program automatically.

Tips and Tricks

Using the Simulated Interface

SimNet XPert uses a *simulated* interface for the *Let Me Try* and *Comprehensive Exercises*. You can open menus without being judged immediately.

Sometimes, depending on how the question is worded, you can open a dialog box and then click **Cancel**, without being judged incorrect. If the question asks you to open a specific dialog box, opening the wrong dialog box will result in "incorrect."

Remember, *Let Me Try* and *Comprehensive Exercises* are scored as "complete" or "incomplete" only. So you can try each step as many times as necessary to get it right.

Working with the Question Box

You can hide the question box by clicking the **Hide Question** button or clicking the minimize arrow at the top right corner of the question box. Click the **Show Question** button to display the question again. If you "lose" the question box, just click the **Show Question** button to show the question box again.

You can also move the question box to another part of the window by clicking the title bar, then dragging the box to its new location.

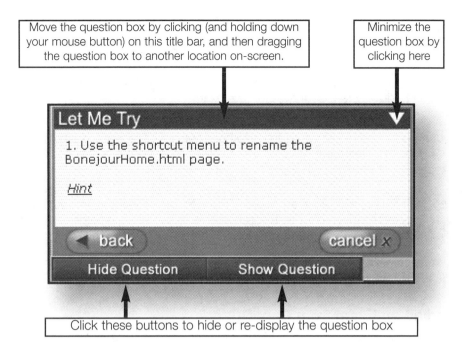

Move the question box by clicking (and holding down your mouse button) on this title bar, and then dragging the question box to another location on-screen.

Minimize the question box by clicking here

Click these buttons to hide or re-display the question box

Showing and Hiding the Let Me Try Question Box

Troubleshooting SimNet XPert Learning

Audio Problems

If you receive errors when displaying the *Show Me* exercises or playing the animations, there is probably a problem with the file associations for your *.wma* audio files.

To fix the problem, re-install the Windows Media Player either from the Windows Media Player 7.0 folder on the **SimNet XPert** CD-ROM or from Microsoft's web site.

SimNet XPert Assessment

Main Menu

The **SimNet XPert Assessment** Main Menu opens after you click the **Take a Test** button. There are three types of exams available:

1. The **Assessment** module Main Menu opens with the *Practice Exams* displayed in the exam list box. *Practice Exams* allow you to practice using the simulated interface, and to test your knowledge. Grades for the default *Practice Exams* are not sent to your instructor.

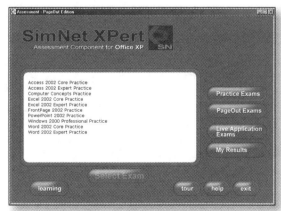

Assessment Component Main Menu

2. To access custom exams your instructor has created, click the **PageOut Exams** button. Using this button is covered in detail in the next section of this documentation: *Loading an Exam from PageOut®.*

3. If you have Microsoft Office XP installed, click the **Live Application Exams** button to display the list of available live exams.

4. The fourth primary button, **My Results**, allows you to access information about your results on the various exams you have taken. For more information on using the **My Results** button, refer to the section later in this manual called *Accessing My Results*.

To begin an exam, click an exam title and then click the **Select Exam** button. Exams can take a minute or two to load, so please be patient if nothing happens at first. You should see a **Loading Exam...** screen within 30 seconds or so.

The **Assessment** Main Menu includes a **Learning** button. You can click this button to go to the **Learning** component.

Loading an Exam from PageOut®

1. Type the **PageOut®** address supplied by your instructor, and then click the **Log In** button. Note that all **PageOut®** addresses end in *.pageout.net*, which is already on the log in screen, so all you need to type is whatever precedes *.pageout.net* in the address supplied by your instructor.

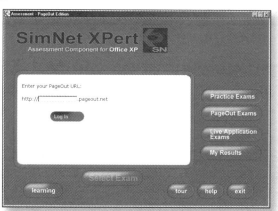

Launching SimNet XPert PageOut® Edition

2. Click the link for your **PageOut®** course from your instructor's **PageOut®** web site home page.

At the instructor's PageOut® Course Web Site

3. Click **SimNet XPert** in the navigation menu at the left side of the next page displayed (or at the bottom of that page), the Course Home Page.

A course home page with SimNet XPert link

4. At the next screen enter your User ID and Password. You should have either received these from your instructor, or you should have been allowed to self-register, in which case you created your own User ID and Password.

The PageOut® Login Screen

5. After logging in successfully you will have access to a menu of exams (and possibly lessons) created by your instructor for you to access. Clicking on an active exam will load that exam on your screen. This may take a few moments, depending on your Internet connection, during which you may still see the Main Menu screen displayed. Please be patient. Within 30 seconds or so you should see a **Loading Exam...** screen.

A brief SimNet XPert menu in PageOut®

Practice Exams

Practice Exams are available for you to go through on your own. The questions are randomly selected, so you may not see the exact same practice exam twice.

Practice Exams are 30 minutes long and allow you to retry questions you answered incorrectly (up to 3 times per question). When you answer a question incorrectly, the program will show a hint telling you how to complete the question.

If you have a McGraw-Hill textbook assigned, the results page will show page numbers for each question. You can print the results page and use the page references as a study guide.

Live Application Exams

Live Application Exams are only available if you have Microsoft® Office XP installed. To start a live exam, click the **Live Application Exams** button on the *Assessment* Main Menu. Click any of the *Live Application Exam* titles to start the test.

In order to complete the live exam, you must answer each question correctly. When you are finished, your score is sent to the Instructor Program for automatic grading.

Accessing *My Results*

Clicking the **My Results** button displays a list of the exams or assessments you have completed which are available for you to view. Your instructor has the ability to delay the displaying of your test results, so a test you took may not appear on this list until the date dictated to SimNet XPert by your instructor.

The My Results menu

To view your results for any available exam, click on the name of that exam and then click the **View Details** button. Doing so displays the end-of-exam results report for that exam. (See the section later in this manual called *Exam Results* for more information on the report itself.)

You can return to the Assessment Component main menu by clicking the **Back to Assessment Main Menu** button. You can go directly to the Learning Component main menu by clicking the Learning button.

Exploring the Simulated Interface

SimNet XPert uses *simulated* application interfaces. You can open menus and (in most cases) open dialog boxes, before the program judges your action as correct or incorrect.

If a question specifies a method for answering the question, you must use the method specified. For example, if the question is "Click the toolbar button to bold the selected text." then pressing CTRL+B on the keyboard would be judged incorrect.

Before taking a custom exam that is graded, we recommend taking one or more of the *Practice Exams* to familiarize yourself with the simulated application interfaces.

Managing the Question Box and Navigating Questions

If you find that the question box covers part of the screen that you need to answer the question, click one of the four corners of the compass graphic in the upper right corner of the question box to move the question box to that corner of the screen. To minimize the question box, click the **Hide** button.

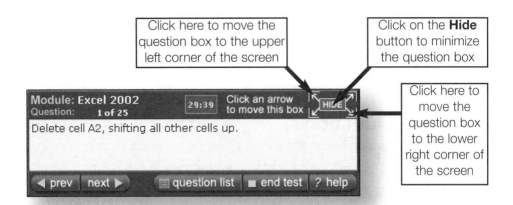

Click here to move the question box to the upper left corner of the screen

Click on the **Hide** button to minimize the question box

Click here to move the question box to the lower right corner of the screen

When the question box is minimized, you'll see this at the bottom of the screen:

Click the *Show* rectangle to show the question box again.

Managing the Assessment Question Box

On the question box you will also find navigation buttons. The **<Prev** button takes you to the previous question on the exam and the **Next>** button takes you to the next question on the exam. You can also move to any question on the exam by clicking the **Question List** button. Clicking on the **Question List** button displays a pop-up menu list all of the question on the exam you are taking, along with a counter showing how many attempts you have already made at answering that question. You can go directly to any question on this list by simply clicking on that question.

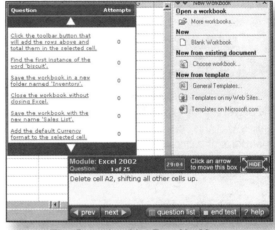

The Question List Pop-Up Menu

Note that you can scroll through the list of questions using the up arrow at the top of the pop-up menu, or using the down arrow at the bottom of the pop-up menu.

Ending an Exam
When you click the **End Test** button on the exam question box, a dialog box will appear with either 2 or 3 options. These options are:

End Exam: clicking this button terminates the exam and sends the results to your instructor for grading.

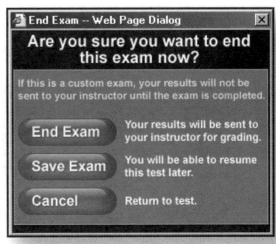

The End Test Dialog Box

Save Exam: clicking this button allows you to pause the exam. You will be able to resume where you left off the next time you access the same exam. (Note that this option can be disabled by your instructor)

Cancel: this option returns you to the exam.

Retaking Questions

If you answer a question incorrectly, you can click the **previous** button at the bottom of the question box to go back and try again. Also, if there is still time, incorrectly answered questions will be repeated at the end of the exam, giving you another chance to answer correctly.

If your instructor has changed the exam preferences so retaking questions is not allowed, once you answer a question incorrectly, you cannot try again.

Feedback and Hints

Usually, you will see **correct** or **incorrect** after you respond to each question. However, if your instructor has disabled the feedback feature, you will not see the feedback, and **SimNet XPert** will advance to the next question automatically.

If hints are enabled, you will see a hint after answering a question incorrectly. If your instructor has disabled the hint feature, you will not see the hints.

Exam Results

When you complete a SimNet XPert exam, an end-of-exam results page may be displayed. Your instructor has the ability to disable this report, or to delay the delivery of this report to your computer. If the results report is enabled by your instructor, it will look similar to the screen you see here.

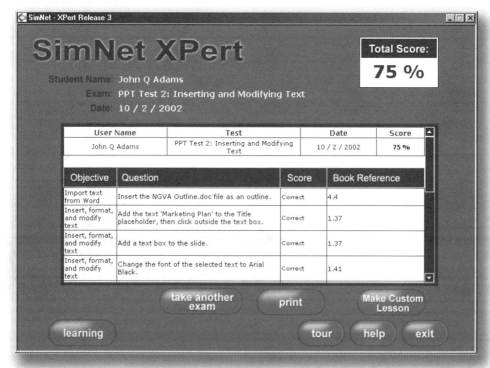

A typical end-of-exam Results Report

Note that in addition to displaying your name, the exam title, the date you completed the exam, and your total score, the report also lists every question on that exam, whether you answered it correctly, incorrectly, or did not attempt to answer it, and a book (page) reference for each question. Your report may not include the book page references if this feature has been disabled by your instructor. If the page references are displayed, you can use them as a "study guide" to refer back to the appropriate page in the McGraw-Hill textbook you are using for your class. That's why you also see a **Print** button on this report; so you can print out your own study guide. (Note that your instructor can also disable the print function, so that button may not appear on the report you see.)

From this screen you can
- go to the Learning Component by clicking the **Learning** button
- return to the Assessment Component Main Menu by clicking the **Take Another Exam** button
- view the product tour by clicking the **Tour** button
- access SimNet XPert help by clicking the **Help** button
- exit SimNet XPert by clicking the **Exit** button
- have SimNet XPert automatically create a custom lesson for you by clicking the **Make Custom Lesson** button. For more on Custom Lessons see the next section of this manual.

Make Custom Lesson

At the end of each exam, there is a **Make Custom Lesson** button. Clicking this button will automatically create a custom lesson based on the questions you did not answer correctly (either answered incorrectly or skipped) in the exam.

1. Click the **Make Custom Lesson** button.

2. Either accept the default name that SimNet XPert suggests for the custom lesson, or type a new name for that custom lesson.

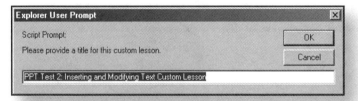

Naming the custom lesson dialog box

3. Click the **OK** button.

4. The next dialog box that appears asks if you want to go directly to the custom lesson that SimNet XPert just created. Click the **OK** button to go directly to the lesson. Click the **Cancel** button to return to the end-of-exam report screen.

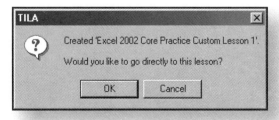

The dialog box asking if you want to go directly to the lesson you just made

If you choose not to go directly to the custom lesson, you can always go to it from the *Learning Component* Main Menu (if you identify your *My Lessons* folder after logging into SimNet XPert).

Changing the Study Guide

The page references that appear in the Book Reference column of your Exam Results report are based on the book you selected during installation for use as the "study guide." You can change the book used at any time from the autorun menu that appears when you insert either of the SimNet XPert CD-ROM's into your CD-ROM drive.

When the autorun menu appears click the "Change My Study Guide Textbook" button.

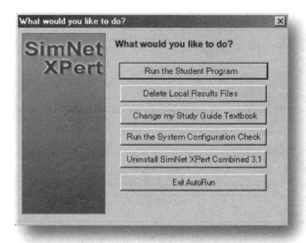

On the next dialog box click the radio button to the left of the textbook you want to use as the new study guide textbook, and click the **Continue** button.

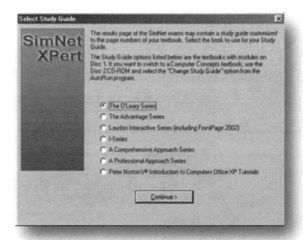

Troubleshooting SimNet XPert Assessment

Live Application Exams Don't Display Questions

If the Office Assistant doesn't appear, or if the Office Assistant doesn't display the *Live Application Exams* question, your macro security settings are set to "high" and the live exam macros can't run.

To set your macro security settings to medium:

1. Click the **Tools** menu, and select **Options...**
2. Click the **Security** tab.
3. Click the **Macro Security...** button.
4. Click the **Medium** radio button. We do not recommend setting your macro security settings to low.
5. Click **OK**. Click **OK** again to close the Options dialog box.

If necessary, close the file and try restarting one of the live exams. Now you should see a message saying that the file contains macros. Click the **Enable Macros** button. Depending on which exercise you open, you may need to enable multiple macros in order for the live exercise to run properly.

You will need to set your macro security settings for Word, Excel, and PowerPoint. Changing the security settings in one application does not affect any of the other Office applications.

Live Application Exams Tips and Tricks

The *Live Application Exams* require that Microsoft Office XP be properly installed on your computer.

Macro Security Warnings

The *Live Application Exams* use macro code (Visual Basic for Applications), which may be disabled if your Office security settings are set too high. Macro security should be set to medium, so you can allow the *Live Application Exams* macros to run. We do not recommend setting the security settings to low.

If You Do Not See the Office Assistant

The live exams use the Office Assistant which may not be enabled on your system. To install the Office Assistant feature, select **Show Office Assistant** from the **Help** menu in the Office application, then follow the instructions that appear. You may need your original Office XP CD-ROM to install the Office Assistant feature.

Technical Support

For up-to-date technical support, check our web site at http://www.simnetxp.net. The web site includes answers to the most frequently asked questions.

You can call Triad Interactive toll free for technical assistance at **1-866-TRIADHELP** or contact us via e-mail at help@triadinteractive.com.

Security, Cookies, and PageOut®

PageOut® requires that you set your browser to accept cookies. Cookies are small files containing text strings that are used to maintain state information as you navigate different pages on a Web site or return to the Web site at a later time. This allows the Web server that uses the cookie to remember the state your browser is in. For example, if you visit Amazon.com and place an order, the Amazon Web server places a cookie on your hard drive that holds information about your user ID, and an ID for each session or visit to the Amazon.com site.

There are actually two different types of cookies: persistent and session cookies. Persistent cookies are placed on your hard drive and remain there until you manually delete them. Session cookies reside in your computer's memory, and are only active during that particular session. Once you terminate that session (as in exiting your browser), session cookies are no longer active. PageOut® only uses session cookies. These session cookies are purely for authentication/security, and do not contain nor collect any specific or personal information about the user whatsoever. What it represents, in a way only intelligible to the PageOut® server, is the user's PageOut® id, and that the user is either an instructor or a student. The cookie does nothing other than represent a specific person and gives them permission to proceed. Although you do not need to have cookies enabled to use PageOut®, if you do not enable cookies you will have to log in again for every protected area.

Setting your browser to allow PageOut's session cookies

Using Internet Explorer 5.5 or 6.0

The most secure way to set your browser to accept the session cookies from PageOut® is to add PageOut® as a "Trusted Site." Doing so tells your browser to accept the session cookie from PageOut® without opening your browser to accepting all third-party cookies.

The steps for setting a Trusted Site in Internet Explorer are the same in either Internet Explorer 5.5 or Internet Explorer 6.0.
1. Start Internet Explorer
2. Click the **Tools** menu
3. Select **Internet Options** from the Tools menu

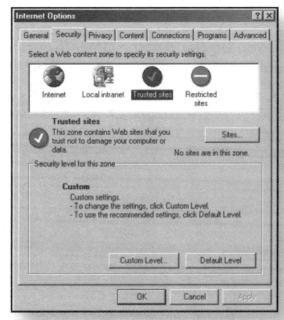

The Internet Options dialog box with Trusted sites selected

4. When the Internet Options dialog box appears, click on the **Security** tab
5. Click the icon representing **Trusted Sites** in the white box beneath the heading: "Select a Web content zone to specify its security settings."
6. Click the **Sites...** button.
7. When the Trusted Sites dialog box appears, type the url for PageOut® in the text box beneath the heading: "Add this Web site to the zone:"
8. If there is a check mark in the box that to the left of the phrase: "Require server verification (https:) for all sites in this zone, click in the check box to remove the check mark (server verification is NOT required for PageOut®).
9. Click the **Add** button.
10. Click the **OK** button on the Trusted Sites dialog box.
11. Click the **OK** button on the Internet Options dialog box.

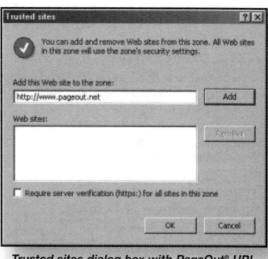

Trusted sites dialog box with PageOut® URL entered and server verification disabled

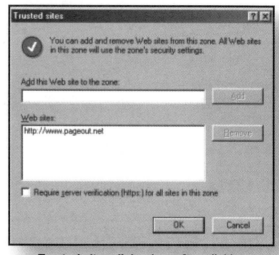

Trusted sites dialog box after clicking the Add button

Virus Protection

Because *SimNet XPert* writes progress files to your hard drive, some virus protection programs may view this action as "malicious." If you see a warning from your virus protection program, allow *SimNet* to run the scripts.

In the example below (Norton Anti-Virus 2002), you would select *Authorize this script*, to allow the TILA (**T**riad **I**nteractive **L**earning **A**rchitecture) program to delete the temporary progress file.

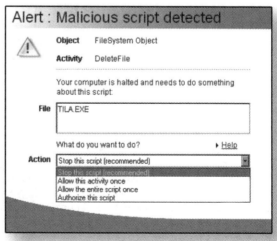

Credits

Triad Interactive, Inc.

SimNet XPert was designed and developed by Triad Interactive, Inc. All content was written by Triad Interactive specifically for this program.

The characters and companies portrayed and the names used in SimNet XPert are fictitious, and any resemblance to the names, character, or history of any person, living or dead, or company is coincidental and unintentional.

Triad Interactive, Inc.
http://www.triadinteractive.com

- Cheryl Manning, Producer
- Catherine Manning, Producer
- William Kohudic, Lead Programmer
- Michelle Martello, Interface and Graphic Design
- Dianne F. Manning, Animations and Graphics
- Timmothy McShane, HTML Programming

- Robert Shortley, HTML Programming
- Adam Stasio, HTML Programming
- Jennifer Gifford, HTML Programming and Graphics
- Matthew Stevens, HTML Programming
- Frank Stasio, Narration
- Charlotte Akin, Narration

Software Engineering by TechRiver:
Dave Townsend, Jim Moore, Greg Brooks, and Jon Singer
email: info@techriver.net

Audio recording and support by EFX Media Services
- Matt Tatusko, Project Manager
- Bruce Dixon, Senior Editor/Engineer
- Marc Magram, Senior Editor

The McGraw-Hill Companies

Published by McGraw-Hill/Technology Education, an operating unit of The McGraw-Hill Companies, Inc., 1333 Burr Ridge Parkway, Burr Ridge, IL 60527. Copyright © 2003 by The McGraw-Hill Companies, Inc. All rights reserved. No part of this publication may be reproduced or distributed in any form or by any means, or stored in a database or retrieval system, without the prior written consent of The McGraw-Hill Companies, Inc., including, but not limited to, network or other electronic storage or transmission, or broadcast for distance learning.

McGraw-Hill Technology Education
http://www.mhhe.com/catalogs/irwin/it/
- Brandon Nordin, Vice President/Publisher, McGraw-Hill/Technology Education
- Bob Woodbury, Editor-in-Chief
- Bill Bayer, Director, New Media Strategies
- Charles Pelto, Manager, Quality Assurance
- Benjamin Curless, Quality Assurance
- Mark Christianson, Manager, Media Technology
- Anthony Sherman, Senior Media Technology Producer
- Gregory Bates, Senior Media Technology Producer
- Jeff Collins, Director, Product Development (PageOut®)
- Scott Criswell, Project Development Project Manager (PageOut®)
- Xin Zhu, Associate New Media Project Manager

Documentation by **Bill Bayer**

©2003 by the McGraw-Hill Companies. All rights reserved.

Appendix A

SimNet XPert Installation
Walk-Through

This appendix walks you through each screen that is displayed during the installation process.

Step 1

What Would You Like to Do?

Once the installation process begins you are asked what you would like to do. Click on the corresponding button depending on your preference: (1) **Install Now,** (2) **View Setup Help,** or (3) **Exit AutoRun**.

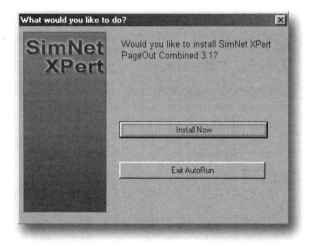

Step 2

Checking System Components

At the next screen you are shown the minimum system requirements for which the setup program will be checking. Click the **Next** button to proceed.

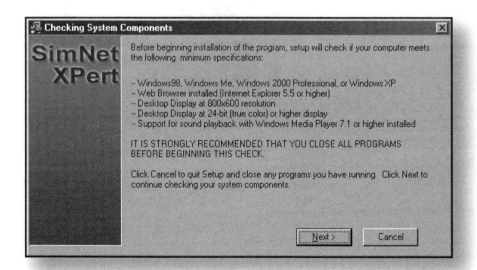

Step 3

Configuration Check Complete

When the setup program has completed the configuration check, you will see the dialog box at the right. Click the **OK** button to proceed.

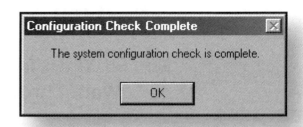

Step 4

License Agreement

On the next screen that appears, read the License Agreement and, if you accept the terms of the agreement, click the **Yes** button.

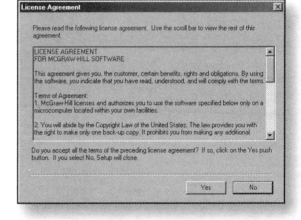

Step 5

Welcome Screen

On the next screen you are encouraged to exit all other Windows programs before continuing the setup process. Click the **Next** button to continue.

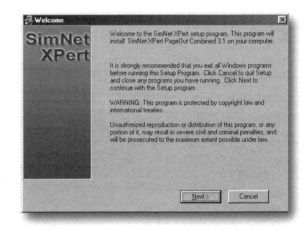

Step 6

Choose Destination Location

On the next screen you need to identify the location on the hard drive where setup will be installing *SimNet XPert*. We strongly recommend that you accept the default location (on the C: drive in a new sub-folder called "SimNet XPert" within your Program Files folder). You can change it, however, if necessary. To change the location, click the **Browse** button and select the new installation location. Click the **Next** button to continue.

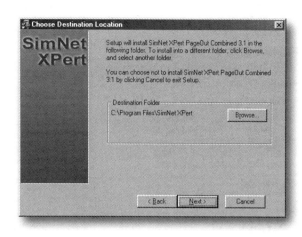

Step 7

Live Exercises

On the next screen you need to specify whether or not the setup program should install the *Live Exercises*. To use the *Live Exercises*, you MUST have Microsoft® Office XP installed on the same computer. If you are unsure if you should install the *Live Exercises*, check with your instructor. Click the **Next** button to continue.

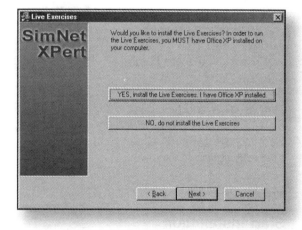

Step 8

Select Textbook and/or Series (1)

On the next dialog box select as many textbooks and/or series you would like by clicking in the check box to the left of that book or series name. This option installs textbook-specific lessons in the SimNet XPert Learning Component. The next screen allows you to select computer concepts text. Click the **Continue** button to proceed.

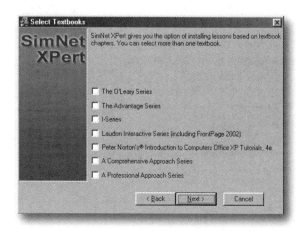

Step 9

Select Textbook and/or Series (2)

On thie dialog box you can select one or more computer concepts text. This option installs textbook-specific lessons in the SimNet XPert Learning Component. Click the **Continue** button to proceed.

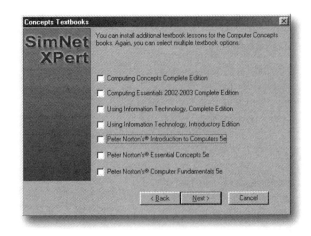

Step 10

Select Program Manager Group

On the dialog box you need to choose the Program Manager group to which *SimNet XPert PageOut®* *3.1* icons will be added. We recommend you go with the default (*SimNet XPert*), but you can select a different existing group from the list, or you can type in the name of a new Program Manager group by selecting the words *SimNet XPert* and typing the name of the new group you want to have created. Click the **Next** button to proceed.

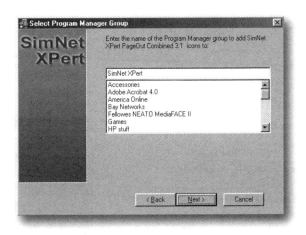

Step 11

Start Installation

You are now ready to begin the installation process. Click the **Next** button to proceed.

On some computers the installation progress bar may appear to be stuck on (or around) 84%. Please be patient.

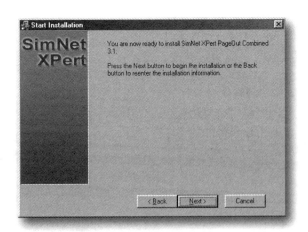

Step 12

Study Guide Selection

On the next screen you need to specify if you want to have a "Study Guide" included on the exam results pages you will see whenever you complete an exam. We recommend that you select a Study Guide upon initial installation. You can always change the Study Guide selection later (after initial installation) when the AutoRun menu appears (when you insert the CD-ROM).

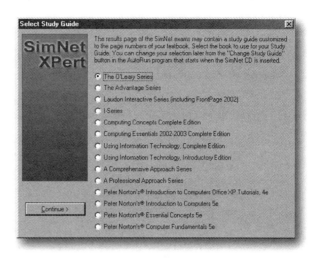

Step 13

Installation Complete

The final screen informs you that the installation has been successful. Click the **Finish** button.

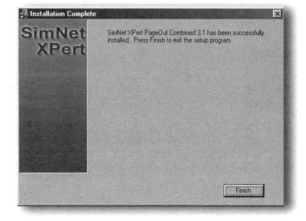

LICENSE AGREEMENT FOR MCGRAW-HILL SOFTWARE

This agreement gives you, the customer, certain benefits, rights and obligations. By using the software, you indicate that you have read, understood, and will comply with the terms.

Terms of Agreement:

1. McGraw-Hill licenses and authorizes you to use the software specified below only on a microcomputer located within your own facilities.

2. You will abide by the Copyright Law of the United States. The law provides you with the right to make only one back-up copy. It prohibits you from making any additional copies, except as expressly provided by McGraw-Hill. In the event that the software is protected against copying in such a way that it cannot be duplicated, McGraw-Hill will provide you with one back-up copy at minimal cost or no charge.

3. You will not prepare derivative works based on the software because that also is not permitted under the Copyright Law. For example, you cannot prepare an alternative hardware version or format based on the existing software.

4. If you have a problem with the operation of our software or believe it is defective, contact your nearest McGraw-Hill Book Company office about securing a replacement. We cannot, however, offer free replacement of software damaged through normal wear and tear, or lost while in your possession. Nor does McGraw-Hill warrant that the software will satisfy your requirements, that the operation of the software will be uninterrupted or error-free, or that the program defects in the software can be corrected. Except as described in this agreement, software is distributed "as is" without any warranties of any kind, either express or implied, including, but not limited to, implied warranties of merchantability and fitness for a particular purpose or use.

5. Additional rights and benefits may come with the specific software package you have purchased. Consult the support materials that come with this program, or contact the nearest McGraw-Hill Book Company office in your area.

NOTICE: THIS PACKAGE IS NOT RETURNABLE IF SEAL IS BROKEN.